10 Steps To Achieving Financial Freedom

Giovanni Dangel

© **Copyright 2016 Giovanni Dangel - All rights reserved.**

This document is geared towards providing exact and reliable information in regards to the topic and issue covered. The publication is sold with the idea that the publisher is not required to render accounting, officially permitted, or otherwise, qualified services. If advice is necessary, legal or professional, a practiced individual in the profession should be ordered.

- From a Declaration of Principles which was accepted and approved equally by a Committee of the American Bar Association and a Committee of Publishers and Associations.

In no way is it legal to reproduce, duplicate, or transmit any part of this document in either electronic means or in printed format. Recording of this publication is strictly prohibited and any storage of this document is not allowed unless with written permission from the publisher. All rights reserved.

The information provided herein is stated to be truthful and consistent, in that any liability, in terms of inattention or otherwise, by any usage or abuse of any policies, processes, or directions contained within is the solitary and utter responsibility of the recipient reader. Under no circumstances will any legal responsibility or blame be held against the publisher for any reparation, damages, or monetary loss due to the information herein, either directly or indirectly.

Respective authors own all copyrights not held by the publisher.

The information herein is offered for informational purposes solely, and is universal as so. The presentation of the information is without contract or any type of guarantee assurance.

The trademarks that are used are without any consent, and the publication of the trademark is without permission or backing by the trademark owner. All trademarks and brands within this book are for clarifying purposes only and are the owned by the owners themselves, not affiliated with this document.

Table of Contents

Introduction 1

Step 1   Don't Work For Money. Let Your Money Work for You 3

Step 2   Being Practical or Being Technical? 8

Step 3   Attitudes Required to Achieve Financial Freedom 10

Step 4   The Art of Leveraging Your Money 13

Step 5   Financial Security 23

Step 6 Financial Comfort 28

Step 7   How to Become Rich Even at a Young Age 32

Step 8   Budgeting and Cost Cutting 43

Step 9   Freelancing and Other Sources of Extra Income 46

Step 10 Dealing with Disappointment 48

Conclusion 60

Introduction

I want to thank you and congratulate you for downloading the book, "10 steps to achieving financial freedom"

This book contains proven steps and strategies on how to achieve financial freedom.

In order to achieve financial freedom, you need to put your money to work, earn passive income, prioritize investment values, choose your partners wisely, deal with disappointment, and trust in the power of your belief.

Whether you want to earn from your investments to help pay for your living expenses or whether you want to invest for the long term so you can achieve the kind of lifestyle that you dream for yourself and your family.

Aside from believing in yourself, trusting yourself is also a very important act that you need to do in order to achieve your financial freedom. If you can't trust yourself, there's no point in establishing your goals and pursuing your dreams.

Once you trust yourself, you are giving yourself the feeling that you are confident, that you can achieve your goals. However, before you can trust yourself, you need to know what you are and who you are.

For instance, if you know that you are easily tempted to buy clothes that you don't actually need, you can acknowledge this weakness and trust yourself that you can change this habit and be more disciplined.

Trust and acceptance go hand in hand to give you the right mindset and provide you with enough energy to chase your dream of financial freedom. When you are confident in yourself and you believe that you can do things, your mind can produce a positive energy that can combat fear, worries, and other negative feelings that are large hurdles in your way towards financial freedom. If you trust all your choices and accept all your decisions, you can be successful in just about anything you want to do.

I hope this 10 steps will guide you to achieve financial freedom.

Let's get started.......

Step 1   Don't Work For Money. Let Your Money Work for You

The idea of working normally places us in a situation where we need to exert great efforts to get money, which in turn means that we have to work for things actively. Once we become passive, we lose the chance to get enough to sustain our preferred lifestyle. This concept is perfectly fine with most people in the world.

However, with this kind of setup, we are just allowing money to "loaf around" or remain idle. After working hard for money, most of us would jump into a spending spree or just keep it in a low-interest bank account. This may be the result of the mindset that there's supposedly no need to invest money, especially if all each one of us needs are several thousand dollars a year. We just love the idea of being comfortable. We don't really aim to be rich.

The technique in investing your money, which means putting your money to work, is not to set aside $100,000 for fancy investments. The technique here is to begin as soon as you can and choose an investment option that combines minimal requirements (especially when it comes to cost) with high revenues.

Once you start investing (even if it's a few dollars a month) and you begin receiving monthly revenues on that investment, you can finally grow your money a hundredfold, even until you notice that you have enough cash to live your life as you want. This is known as compound growth, and it allows your small investment to become a trove of wealth, in time. For example, if you have a $200 investment that earns you 20% on a monthly basis, you can have $1,486.015 in 12 months, $ 13,249.475 in 24 months, and $118,133.645 in 36 months. Even if you generate slightly smaller revenues, you will still greatly benefit from your passive investment. To make your money work for you and to achieve sustainable profits, you need to set aside a few dollars to make an investment. You should also allocate a few hours a week for your moneymaking pursuits. Finding a dependable investment tool that can help your money grow is also a must.

Investment Is Not Just For Rich People

For those people who have spent most of their lives playing the rat race, the idea of putting money to work is almost a strange concept. After all, the common mindset is that once you have money, you need to spend it on your personal (or your family's) needs, such as food, clothes, and shelter. When you have some spare cash, that's the time when you buy something not really necessary, such as expensive clothes, jewelry, and movie tickets. If there's still money left after you've satisfied your urge for luxury or entertainment, you can make a deposit in a low-interest account.

Being rich can be your choice. Why choose to be an average person if you also have the chance to reap the rewards of wealth. All you need to do is to learn how to make your money work for you, rather than spending all your time and energy to get money.

Start Today

It is totally wrong to think that it is too late to begin investing. There's no better time to begin earning profits than today. After all, if you don't start as soon as you can, the amount that you'll manage to earn would turn out to be much smaller. As business gurus say, time is money. However, that doesn't mean that you have to get your money from the bank right now and invest all of it abruptly. What you can do today is find the best investment options available, so that you can choose and decide according to your preferences.

For example, you can visit banks in your area and inquire about high-yielding deposits that you can afford. You can also learn about the stock market, gold investment, and other options that you could try for the sake of making your money work for you. You must also find ways to shield your investments against the effects of recessions.

Save and Invest Smartly

In achieving financial freedom, it is best to invest as wisely as you can and save as much as you can. Saving, though, can be really demanding. First, you need to spend less than what you earn while working longer to increase your income. Second, you must be free of the kinds of debt that you can live without, such as the ones that stem from your shopping sprees.

Once you have enough savings to make small investments, you could finally invest smartly. There's no sense in saving your money for investments, only to have it vanish into thin air because you have failed to understand what you're getting into and you didn't make the right decisions in managing your finances.

You can easily find numerous resources on the matter of making smart investments. You can take advantage of the available resources to become an expert in making investments. Soon enough, you will realize that putting your money to work is actually easy, once you know how to do it.

Step 2   Being Practical or Being Technical?

Since the topic of financial independence is broad, the approaches for the achievement of financial independence are also broad. Let us take a look at the practical and technical practices in achieving financial independence.

Practicality Defined

The word practical can mean many things. These are:

- Relating to reality
- Appropriate or suitable for use in actual situation
- Reasonable to do or use
- Likely to succeed
- Manifests in practice or action
- Being in effect or actively engaged in course of action
- Capable of being put to use
- Qualified for practical training or practice
- Hence, practicality is the application of the things listed above.

Technicality Defined

Technicality covers a wide scope. Hence it includes:

- Relating to practical use of science or machines
- Teaching skills rather than ideas
- Special knowledge on how a machine works or how particular work is done
- Relating to technique

Practicality vs. Technicality

Practicality may pertain to the management of what you already have. For example, you have a fixed income of $100. To obtain financial independence, that is to have your income higher than your expenses, you must do something to control expenses. This includes budgeting, cost-cutting, setting your priorities or taking excessive leisures out of your life.

On the other hand, technicality covers the procedure to attain or achieve something. For example, you have affixed income of $100. In order to obtain financial independence, you will resort to activities which you think will increase your income. These activities may take the forms of investments, management of borrowings, applying for insurances and doing other jobs aside from your primary source of living.

Step 3   Attitudes Required to Achieve Financial Freedom

Financial freedom is not a matter of how much your wealth is, or how much money is waiting for you when you finally decided to retire. It is more about the self- fulfilling feeling of being satisfied with how your money works for you and your necessities. Here are the key attitudes needed to achieve financial freedom.

Commitment

Being committed means having you involved in or dedicating yourself to a specific matter. This is to be taken together with the obligation. This force drives you to set goals on how to achieve the desired result. If you are not committed to what you are doing, the foundation of your desire for the achievement of the goal is weak.

The same is true with the commitment to achieve financial freedom. This is not just about telling yourself that you want to be financially independent. It is more about driving yourself to take action to achieve your desired results. This is also a long-term contract.

Self-Discipline

If you have already decided to commit yourself to attain financial freedom, it does not end there. It is a mere drive; hence, it should be accompanied with action. This action is what we call self-discipline. This term is associated with self-control.

Self- control is the capacity to control behavior, desires or emotion to perform a function, particularly relating to self or society. Psychologically speaking, this also pertains to self- regulation. This is an essential step in achieving goals and avoiding impulses or emotions that may hinder the achievement of goals.

Necessity over Luxury

This attitude is important in achieving financial freedom. More often than not, we are preoccupied with our wants which have already exceeded our needs. We tend to spend or crave luxurious items when, in reality, they have cheap equivalents with the same purpose or quality.

In order to effectively manage your money, you should know what to do or buy and what to not do or not buy. This will help you choose better alternatives.

Effective Management of Resources

This attitude will help you with the effective utilization of your given resources. It takes planning to determine whether your money will be productive if invested in certain activities. It also takes careful weighing of opportunities and cost before allowing your money to leave your hands.

In many cases, people with sufficient resources tend to fail in becoming financially independent. This is because of the confidence regarding sufficiency. People with limited resources tend to succeed in becoming financially independent because of the challenge of lacking sufficiency.

Step 4   The Art of Leveraging Your Money

When you begin earning money, start to consider ways of leveraging it. You must learn the art of saving small sums of money for you to gather larger amounts. Some people willingly accept debt just to buy luxurious products that are not really valuable. If you are young and you still haven't started a family of your own, you need to lay the foundation today so you can reap financial rewards in the next decade.

For example, as early as now, you can learn about using options to buy real estate, so that when the time comes that you want to buy a house, you will easily know what to seek. Starting today, you must also learn to spend less. Save at least 15 to 20% of your monthly income, so that you will have enough funds for your investments. Also, you should learn to get value for money from your favorite products and services.

Here's something that's both interesting and alarming – 90% of people are enticed by advertisements into becoming real customers. They end up availing of products and services that are merely for entertainment. The smarter

10% are more imaginative, creative, and logical, so they avoid making unnecessary expenses. They're normally the ones who generate wealth by doing something they really love.

Game developers, writers, and software developers are the best examples of those who work hard initially, then relax while earning royalties for their creations.

Meanwhile, if you have a unique vision, discipline, determination, and guts, you can even start your own company. Google, which is now the leading search engine, was founded in a dorm room. Similarly, Apple, the number one company in the consumer electronics niche, was started in a garage. These two companies are now worth billions of dollars.

You must be aware that we are living in an age where creativity, imagination, and great ideas could be easily marketed. There's no need to follow the traditional path of establishing a business. The World Wide Web is an endless space where people are becoming richer and richer, particularly through the power of leveraging.

Of course, there's no harm in trying out new things. For instance, you can invest in real estate or in certain stocks. If you choose the latter, you can begin with stocks that are starting out – those that are in the $10 to $20 range. Afterward, learn all about the industry, the company, as well as its products and services. Maximize your intellect as well as your intuition.

Finally, don't loaf around if you want to make money. The fact that you want your money to work for you doesn't give you the license to be totally idle. You also need to exert effort.

The Power of Passive Income

Earning passive income is the key to making money work for you. Even though it is impossible that you will earn millions in several days, taking advantage of several sources of passive income is a great way to make more money (especially if you still have an active source of income).

Interests Earned from Bank Accounts and Deposits

The job market is becoming more and more unstable. There's no assurance that you will still have your current job in the next few months. Hence, it makes a lot of sense to explore additional sources of passive income. Earning money from several jobs can establish a safety net, which could shield you from the consequences of losing a job. It can also provide you a lot of financial freedom, particularly if you need to pay a lot of bills.

Passive income will generate profit despite not being an actual job. You just need to exert effort during the initial stages so you can enjoy the continuous flow of income later. Earning enough income and expanding your passive wealth will thin out your vulnerabilities when it comes to your finances. It can also help you in building a fat bank account. Below are some secrets in building passive wealth in the comforts of your own home.

Open a High-Interest Bank Account

A great way of making money work for you is by opening a bank account that yields high interest. For example, if you have $4,000 that you want to invest, you can increase your money by almost 20%. Most low-interest accounts can only give you a maximum of 5%. In order to find out which bank can offer you the best rates, you may need to consult a bank officer and ask about the terms and conditions that come with a high-yield account.

The great thing is that most banks today are into online banking, so you can take advantage of the best rates. Meanwhile, you can also choose to bank with financial institutions that are completely online. These online banks don't need to pay for the upkeep of their offices, so their operational expenses are essentially minimum. As a result, they can provide higher interest to their depositors.

Dividends from Stocks and Bonds

In stocks investment, you can earn a dividend based on the performance of your chosen stocks. Once you buy stocks, you will be paid a portion of what the company is receiving as profit, as long as the stock market is high. The earnings received by a stockholder from the investment are often referred to as "dividends." These are usually paid out to encourage investors to purchase more stocks. Because there are several risks, this type of investment should be taken with careful consideration.

Primarily, you need to research stock options. Before you can make any type of stock investment, you need to take a closer look if the company is paying dividends or not. You must do this because not all companies pay their stockholders in dividends. A good way to determine whether a company is paying dividends is to consult the Wall Street Journal. You could register for an online account to monitor firms that are paying dividends.

The obvious risk that comes with stock dividends lies in whether the company would be able to pay the investors continuously. If the company is not performing well, there's a bigger probability that it would not pay its investors, even annually. You need to find companies that can pay their investors at least quarterly. It is best to find a company that regularly increases its dividends and is not cutting its dividends from time to time.

Although you may not be comfortable with judging a company based on its activities in the past, checking the background of the company (particularly the dividends payout) is still recommended. After evaluating the background of the company and you've learned that it is reliable in paying dividend stocks, you can finally decide whether you'd like to earn from that company. It is best to review the company payout at least five years back or more.

Another strategy to use when you are searching for dividend stocks to invest in is checking the dividend yield of the company. This refers to the percentage that reflects both the present price and the availability of shares. To put it simply, the yield refers to how much money you can earn from the investments you have made on your dividends. Find a yield that can provide you profits of at least 3%.

Income from Rental Property

Another source of passive income is through renting out your property. It will not take that much to transform yourself from being a regular homeowner into someone who makes a profit by renting out property. If you need to move but you want to keep your old home, rent it out instead of selling it.

Although many people would want to have an extra home to rent out, getting into the rental property business can be stressful. You need to determine if your property is worth renting out and you need to consider the people who want to be your tenants. Your home for rent should be in good condition, in a strategic place, and its mortgage must already be paid off. You can charge a higher rent as long as your abode has these qualities.

Another factor that you must consider is if your character is well suited for the task. You first need to evaluate yourself and find out whether you have the time and the skill to manage the business properly. Aside from your obligation to yourself in keeping the business afloat, you also need to provide a safe place for your tenants. This means that you need to make certain that the property has proper wiring, plumbing, and air conditioning, among others. You also need to make sure that the stairs are safe and the structure is strong enough to shield your tenants from external harm. Meanwhile, you need to study the state laws and policies on rental properties, such those about advertising the place, choosing renters, and evicting delinquent tenants.

If you are already in this kind of business, you can easily stand out. There are so many conventional rental properties out there and most property owners seem to be doing the same monotonous things. If you'd choose to be unique, you could considerably increase your profits. One unique thing you can do is add more options to increase the rent. If your budget allows it, you can hire a landscape artist to transform the yard into a garden. You can also avail of the services of a cleaning company to make certain that the house will be clean. These things will make your property more presentable to your potential tenants, as well as make high rents reasonable.

Income from Intellectual Property

In the last decade, the determination and valuation of intangible properties, particularly intellectual property have caught the attention of many for different reasons. This includes high compliance requirements for easy financial reporting. It's also important to note that there are opportunities for leveraging your money because financial organizations gradually embraced alternative sources for collateral.

Basically, intellectual property refers to creations that come from a person's mind, realized through the creation of records (such as writing) and associated with legal rights (such as trademark, copyright, and patent). You can earn royalties from books, films, paintings, photographs, software, and other creations.

Mere ideas don't qualify as intellectual property. The intellectual property law protects the expression of this idea. For instance, you can't claim the idea behind a novel as your own intellectual property, but you can copyright the novel that you have written, which in turn grants you exclusive rights for the book.

Because intellectual property is very easy and cheap to reproduce, particularly if it is in digital form, it is a good source of passive income. You can provide value to your target audience by copying and sharing data, which can be automated. Once you become successful in creating a high-value intellectual property, you can sit back, relax, and enjoy the royalties.

Creating a piece of intellectual property involves a great deal of work, but this "work" can be done during the initial stage. Afterward, you can then reproduce or duplicate the property, so that you can distribute it or share it with your audience. You can still earn passive income half a century from now for an intellectual property that you've created today.

For example, you can compose music today and then earn income from the direct sales of your album or from the royalties given by the recording studio. You can also earn money when the music is used in theatrical and film productions.

Step 5   Financial Security

It is a great achievement to become financially secure because you don't need to worry about money. However, it's best to remember that people define financial security differently.

Try asking at least 10 people about their definition of financial security, as well as their thoughts on when they'd achieve that status. There's a high chance that you will get 10 different answers. For you, financial security might be having $1 million in the bank, while for some, $10 Million is not enough.

With today's economy, having $1 million in the bank is not what it used to be. Just try paying your mortgage in full, and you will be left with a few thousand dollars. Even keeping a million dollars intact in the bank will only yield 3%. So, it could only earn you an annual income of $30,000, which is not enough if you want to rub shoulders with billionaires. Well, if you have $10 million, you can earn $300,000 every year without doing anything at all.

However, the problem in defining financial security through these terms is that raking in millions is almost an impossible dream for most of us. Certainly, you want a million dollars in your bank account, and there's nothing wrong to aim for that goal. The downside of defining financial security through millions of dollars is that it gives you the idea that you're gunning for something impossible. Rather, we must use a more realistic definition of financial security, which can be achieved whether you are making $10,000 or $10,000,000 annually.

It can also be beneficial to take a look at what financial security is not. It is not all about producing a specific amount of money. There are people out there who have earned millions of dollars, but they are not yet financially secure. I'm sure you have heard of actors, athletes, and lottery winners who ended up being bankrupt. If you made $1 Million and you have spent $1.5 million, don't consider yourself financially secure.

Financial security is also not limited by having a villa – with servants bringing you wine while you spend a lazy hot afternoon by your infinity-edge pool. If you choose that lifestyle, there's nothing wrong about it, but this can be a very limited definition of what being financially secure is.

We need a broader definition of financial security, which puts the status within the reach of anyone who wants to attain a better financial situation. You can call yourself financially secure if you meet the following four criteria:

- You have zero debts
- You can control your expenses
- You can regularly increase your savings
- You don't need to keep a job you don't want
- You aren't satisfied with making make ends meet

1. You have zero debt

Minimal debt can be understandable. You may borrow from a bank to buy your own car or a new home. Getting a loan for your education is very acceptable. However, getting into debt to buy luxury clothing is not.

If you have credit cards and have a habit of using it, maybe you are still paying for the vacation you took years ago or an elegant, romantic dinner that cost you a month's salary, or a gadget that could easily become obsolete in just a matter of months.

Bear in mind that when you are indebted to someone, you essentially give that person power over you. This is because you need to pay that individual back. If you refuse to pay, you could end up facing legal troubles. You could lose the things that are dear to you, such as your car or home, because they can be sequestered by the bank. Meanwhile, if you borrowed money from your friends or relatives and you can't pay them back, you could also lose their trust.

2. Controlling your expenses

If your expenses are higher than your earnings, you are on your way to being poor. If you control your expenses so they don't go over your income, you can save the extra money and you can be on your way to becoming financially secure.

3. Increase Your Savings Regularly

Many of us have little savings, despite having worked for decades. For numerous reasons, some people cannot save money because they burn through their paychecks. The key here is to focus on saving money each month. You can experience great satisfaction if you watch your savings grow, particularly because the interest could compound and become a passive source income even if you didn't intend for it to be one.

4. Not Working on a Job that You Don't Like Just to Make Ends Meet

A large percentage of the workforce survives from payday to payday, stuck in a not-so-desirable career just to make ends meet. Once people resign from their jobs (or they lose their jobs), it will take several months before they can patch up things.

Once you have zero debts, control your expenditures, and concentrate on increasing your monthly savings, you can easily survive most financial hardships, such as losing your job. You will also have the freedom to change your career, because you can find a job that you want without suffering financial troubles.

Financial security is an achievable goal that can be pursued by anyone. However, it is crucial to get a clear definition of financial security, so that you can have higher chances of achieving it.

Step 6 Financial Comfort

Financial security is a short-term goal, which can be achieved within five to 10 years. On the other hand, financial comfort is a life-long goal, which could be achieved by being financially secure for decades. To put it simply, you cannot be financially comfortable if you are not financially secure. Becoming financially comfortable is the next step in the financial ladder.

Like what we did in defining financial security, it is also crucial to determine what it means to be financially comfortable. Before you delve deeper, it is essential to determine precisely what financial comfort is. If you are thinking that you are financially comfortable because you have spare money in the bank, you are wrong. This is more about becoming satisfied on how you are managing your life, with enough money at your disposal. This means being able to do the things that you want without being hurdled because of money issues.

Achieving financial comfort depends primarily on understanding the link between the amount of money you need against the demands of your life, which are basically categorized into three - basic, entertainment, and savings. Basic expenses refer to food and shelter. Entertainment expenses refer to vacations, hobbies, and luxury items. Savings expenses refer to the extra money you set aside each month so that you can have enough funds during emergencies or when retirement finally comes.

To be financially comfortable, you need to decide what type of retirement lifestyle you want. With the above definition, it is clear that deciding on what type of lifestyle you'd want to enjoy could depend on the amount of money that you are saving now.

Lifestyle preferences are individual-oriented in nature. Some people are happy with having the necessities, so they are very frugal. Others want to see the world by traveling, partying, and engaging in new ventures. There are also people who want to keep on working because they are in love with their careers. Being precise in defining the kind of life you want to live once you reach your retirement age can help you determine how much money you need to set aside.

You could speak to a financial consultant, sign up for a state-regulated pension account, or read online resources to properly work your way towards retirement. This means that you need to take a more precise approach to planning your retirement.

It is also crucial to decide when you want to retire. This is an important decision because it has a big impact on your savings. If you want to retire early, you need to make serious decisions about your retirement plans. However, if you are willing to work until you are 70 or 80 years old, you have enough time to acquire the funds you need when you decide to stop working and finally enjoy the rest of your life.

What you can do today is to review your present saving options. Probably, you have already opened a bank account to deposit your savings. This is a great move. However, it can be beneficial to check the saving options you have with your current bank to make certain that it is the best option for you. Take a look at the interest rates, and check whether you are getting the best deal or you need to consider exchanging your savings account with tax-free products, so that you can earn more while saving. Also, check all the savings you have, to determine if they can provide you with enough returns to achieve your financial goals.

Planning for your comfortable retirement can be a daunting task. Some people even experience anxiety because they have been able to identify their goals, but cannot achieve them. In spite of learning more about financial security and the importance of retirement planning, not all people have the confidence and the discipline required to achieve financial goals. Hence, it is recommended to consult an expert.

A professional financial advisor can guide you through all the options – with the help of the latest information, as well as projections in terms of how much you need to save each month. You can be exposed to financial advice that you may have never heard before, which can help you increase your savings at a much faster rate.

Take note that in order for you to retire in financial comfort you must think long term. While the specific figures may vary, financial advisors believe that a luxurious lifestyle can be achievable if your income during your retirement reaches the range of $50,000 per year. For you to attain this, you need to save at least $1000 per month, which can be unrealistic for some people.

Certainly, there are many other ways to save money and your financial advisor can explain these things to you. However, the fact remains that the earlier you begin saving, the more funds you'll have access to and the more comfortable your retirement will be. Simply put, you should start saving today.

Step 7 How to Become Rich Even at a Young Age

The first thing you need to do to become rich is to change the way you think about money. Many of us maintain a love-hate relationship with wealth. We may be jealous of those who have accumulated a lot of wealth, but may spend our whole life chasing money. The primary reason why most people cannot gather enough money is because they are not well aware of its nature as well as its life-changing potential.

Similar to a person, money is a living thing. When you go to work, you are actually marketing a product - yourself, particularly the services and skills you can provide to your employer. In the same case, your assets (including your money) can also wake up each morning and has the potential to work. This is the key in accumulating wealth. Every dollar that you save should be considered as an employee. In due time, the main goal is to encourage your dollars to work hard, and gradually, they can make enough money so that you can have more cash. Once you become successful, you don't need to sell your own services. Instead, you can live off the labor of your money.

The next thing to do is to understand the strength of small amounts. Most people follow the wrong notion that they should start with millions of dollars to make a lucrative income. These people are actually suffering from a "not enough" mindset because if they cannot make thousands of dollars in investments, they cannot be rich. However, these people don't realize that even a large desert is made grains of sands. Many success stories feature people who have saved every dollar and have been frugal before they became wealthy. Don't underestimate the idea of starting small.

Bear in mind that with every dollar you save, you can buy yourself freedom. Once you tune into this mindset, you will see that spending $20 for unnecessary things can make a considerable difference in the long run. Because money has the ability to work and provide you with earnings, the more money you have, the faster and larger it could grow. When you have money, you can be free. You can reap the rewards of freedom by staying at home with your children instead of working countless hours, or you can visit places around the world without worrying that you might lose your job. If you are earning from any source now, you can start building your own wealth. Maybe you can start with a dollar.

Every investment you make can be a grain you can use to buy out your financial freedom.

Also, take note that you are responsible for what is happening in your life. Some people don't want to invest in stocks because they don't want to wait long years just to become rich, so they would rather enjoy money today by spending it. The downside of this mindset is that there's the possibility that you are going to be still alive in the next 10 to 20 years. The main concern here is whether you will be financially independent in the future. An important task that you must do today is to prepare your finances.

If you are interested in making investments, be certain to buy stocks instead of certain products. Most rich people in the United States generate 30% of their income from investments put into stocks. This is the reason why they are becoming richer and richer as time goes by. Once you conquer the challenge of financial slavery by changing the way you spend your money, and with the right discipline and determination, you can be rich.

To be rich, you must learn how to become one by learning about the people who have achieved lasting wealth. It is best to emulate the attributes that you admire from your icon and just ignore the ones that may be negative. Start molding yourself into who and what you want to become. Choose to invest into yourself first, and you will realize that money will just come. Success and wealth will only lead to greater success and wealth. You need to buy that freedom, and you can do that by putting your money to work.

However, you must understand that getting more money is not the only way to become rich. Acquiring more money cannot solve all your problems. If you do not perform well in a job that pays you $20,000 per year, how can you possibly handle a job that provides you with six-figure salaries? The latter can bring out the worst in you. Many people out there are even earning $100,000 monthly and yet they're still trying to survive from payday to payday. The problem is not the figures on your paycheck. The way you handle money could make or break your life.

It is said that insanity is doing similar things over and over again and expecting different results. If your parents today are not living the life you prefer, then break the cycle and don't do what they did. Follow the road less traveled and break away from the norms of your ancestors – that is, if you want a different life for yourself. Unless your parents are wealthy and know how to handle their wealth, do something for yourself by looking for another way to maximize your life.

For you to achieve the financial freedom that you want, you need to accomplish two things. First, you need to commit yourself to clearing your debts. Second, save regularly and save a lot. Purchasing equity is important in building your wealth. You can become rich if you invest your money into a business with lucrative long-term revenues.

Once you finally made the choice to be rich, the prospect of retiring the way you want (financial comfort) and doing what you want today (financial security) will just follow. Today, make the choice of controlling your life by working hard for money and later on putting your money to work for you. When you strategically create these stepping stones, every day that passes will drive you closer to your ultimate goal - financial freedom.

It is also best to adjust your mindset. Treat every dollar that comes into your wallet like a seed that you can grow for your financial future. If you are responsible and you have the determination and the discipline, financial success will come to you naturally.

Choosing Your Partners Wisely

Choosing your partner in life well is definitely crucial. Setting aside the romantic perspective, choosing the person whom you will spend the rest of your life must be taken seriously, because you need to find someone who understands your goals and will help you realize your dreams.

Money problems are among the top reasons why couples file for divorce. Certainly, lack of money can damage the relationship, especially if the couple cannot make ends meet. However, excessive money can also shatter relationships, especially if the couples do not know how to handle money or they don't have matching views in establishing financial goals and in choosing moneymaking strategies.

Similar to marriage, choosing your business partners is also a crucial decision. After all, you need to find people whom you can trust your money with and whom you can share your vision, ideals, and aspirations to, particularly on why you want to become wealthy.

In choosing your business partners, there are two rules that you need to follow:

- Never pick a partner who needs money
- Never give equity to a person whose services you can get from the marketplace

Certainly, most people who want to establish businesses want money because they want to be rich. Some of them wish to further expand their wealth. However, in choosing your partners, don't go for those who are in need of money, because there's a risk that they will make important decisions for the company by simply thinking about finances, instead of looking at the bigger picture. If you have spotted a person with a talent or skill that can be crucial to your business, then get that individual as an employee – not as a partner. This is particularly true if other people can also provide services that are essentially the same as those offered by that person.

What Makes Good Business Partners?

Good partners have aligned values, and they are people that help you enjoy whatever it is that you're doing.

Aligned Values

One of the early stages of establishing your own business is to define your values. Many successful business owners today defined their values while they were still establishing their strategies and forging different kinds of partnerships.

The primary goal is to define your values and translate them into action. To put it simply, you need to answer the question of "what will your partners experience as those values are expressed?" However, personal values and company values may not align with each other at all times.

More often than not, aligning values with your business partners is not something that can happen naturally. There is a need to forge it by being on the same page and by establishing a strong commitment to shared strategic goals and achievable purposes. Even though you are partners, it is also important to be clear on who will be the leader. Not choosing someone who'd boss others around, but to define the person who needs to set the vision, direct the business, and establish the culture in the company.

This strong commitment from partners is important in developing effective and sustainable working relationships based on openness, transparency, and dedication to solving problems.

It is also best to clarify the parameters for the collaboration and identify the roles and responsibilities of each partner. There is also a need for business partners to invest time and resources, to grow the business according to their aligned values.

Generosity

It is true that establishing your own business can help you become rich. For that reason, you may be wondering why there is a need to find generous partners. After all, you are establishing a for-profit organization and not a charitable institution.

Generosity is among the most important qualities that people usually look for in their leaders. This is not just about generosity in terms of money, though. Research shows that there are other important things to partners, especially in what they hope to see from their leaders. You can be generous in terms of not only money, but also when it comes to information, power, credit, time, faith, and trust. It is really difficult to work with someone who seems to be always trying to compete, and who doesn't believe in others' potentials.

Having too many partners over the years encourage competition, thinking that if people in the business will try hard to beat each other, it will improve their skills and eventually make them better. However, this could be risky because it can backfire. When partners are trying to compete with each other, trust could go downhill, communication could be shattered, and outstanding ideas may be blocked. Also, the valuable energy you need to run your business could be spent in sabotaging each other.

The Importance of Working with People You Like

People who are satisfied with their jobs tend to be more dedicated, better organized, and perform faster. Numerous studies have also been conducted, suggesting that businesses with satisfied partners usually perform better than businesses with disgruntled partners.

If you are running your business and you are ignoring the satisfaction of your partners, you may be making a large mistake. In a 2010 study published in the Journal of Vocational Behavior, it has been revealed that how people feel about their colleagues at work can largely affect their job satisfaction. An interesting note about this study is that it shows that satisfaction doesn't only exist in a professional sense, but also manifests in the form of everyday satisfaction in life. If you are working with people you enjoy being around with, you will have a higher chance of being satisfied with your job, and eventually, you can be more satisfied with your life. This can give you the feel-good attitude, which is important in building your wealth.

The study also revealed that the effect of being satisfied at work matters more to some people. For instance, if you are naturally generous, warm, collaborative, and trusting, you usually have an agreeable personality. The study revealed that the relationships between satisfaction of colleagues, job satisfaction, and life satisfaction were even more important to people who are very agreeable.

The effect of job satisfaction on individuals is very clear. If you are working with people you hate, there is the high chance that you also don't like your job, and it has implication on how you view your life. Working with people you enjoy being around with is crucial.

Step 8 Budgeting and Cost Cutting

In this step, some of the practical ways of achieving financial freedom will be discussed. This chapter will focus on budgeting and cost-cutting.

Budgeting

It is a plan to be used as a guideline for saving and spending purposes. The key factor in budgeting is to know where your money is allotted and to spend less than what you earn. An effective budget plan can ensure that you pay bills on time, achieve financial goals and make room for contingencies.

Principles of Budgeting

Conservatism

In budgeting, you must understand the actual results, in some cases, may vary from the planned results. Since budgeting is a forecast, it does not render absolute assurance. In doing a budget, you must put a margin, which is more effective if you underestimate your income and overestimate your expenses. Therefore, you can make room for possible contingencies.

Preparation Time

Budgeting cannot and should not be done within a few hours. An ample time is necessary to weigh what to include and what to omit, so that an efficient and the effective budget plan will be produced. Also, the budget plan must be flexible and include the possibility of new information affecting it. Consultations and research are essential parts of budgeting.

Cost-Cutting

These are the measures implemented to decrease expenses:

Writing down your daily expenses

Keeping track of your expenses is not a hard job. All you need is a handy notebook to list all of your expenses daily. You must also list the costs to be paid on a monthly basis, such as utilities and rent. From you record, you can now easily identify the costs to be cut off or regulated.

Cut down utilities

In order to lessen your expenses, you must know how to save, not only money, but resources. If you are spending a lot on water, electricity and phone bills, minimize their usage. You can do simple things such as turning off the faucet while brushing your teeth; turning off the lights when not in use; avoid phone chatting when not necessary, and recycle water when watering plants or washing your car.

Step 9 Freelancing and Other Sources of Extra Income

You must not rely only on your primary source of income. You must also find jobs that will give you extra income without sacrificing your quality of work on your primary source; some of which are part- time jobs, freelancing and other sources of extra income.

Part-Time Jobs

Aside from working 8 hours a day in an office or any other work, which gives rise to your primary income, you can also find part- time jobs which only requires about a portion of your time. In this manner, you have a sure and guaranteed earnings derived from your primary work and an additional income from your part- time job.

Your income from your primary job may cover living expenses and necessities. On the other hand, your income from part- time jobs may take part of your savings or allocation for contingencies.

Freelancing

Due to fast changing technology and globalization, there are many jobs offered as a freelance job. Freelance worker or freelancer refers to a person who is not necessarily committed to a specific employer for a long-term setup. Also, it refers to someone who is self-employed. Often, freelancers are represented by an agency that resells their labor. One of the most popular freelancing jobs nowadays is the freelance writing. Because of the growing demand of contents for online sites and other media, there is a high demand for freelance writing. Your hard work and determination will be the basis of your earnings.

Business Venture

Aside from working, you can also join business ventures or create one. The advantage is that you have the full control on how the business works. Your profit or loss is based on how you plan and strategize. Also, business ventures are one of the most successful ways to become rich.

Step 10 Dealing with Disappointment

Setting your financial goals and trying hard to achieve them can be very stressful, particularly if you don't know how to deal with disappointments. Disappointment is an emotion that most of us who want to achieve financial freedom may have a hard time understanding and managing. For instance, when you've purchased stocks and later on the company goes bankrupt to the point of not paying returns, it can be a blow to you. However, just like any emotion, disappointment can be controlled. In fact, you can turn this emotion into an opportunity to learn.

Successful People Face and Learn from Disappointment

On your journey towards financial success, you will definitely face disappointments in different scales. As a matter of fact, the more you want to achieve your financial goals, the larger the risk you face of being disappointed. However, what matters is how you deal with it. Dealing with disappointment can even become an alternative way of becoming successful. It can teach you how to be patient, how to learn from your setbacks, and accept the reality that life can be sometime painful and unfair.

It can be easy to perceive disappointment as a failure on your part, because it can really feel so bad. Your first reaction may be to soothe yourself and sulk in a corner. You may just grab a tub of ice cream, sleep for hours, or try to drink away the bad feelings. Although these things are not actually bad, they can be dangerous if you choose to sulk for long periods.

In dealing with financial disappointments, you need to face things and move past the emotion. It is true that disappointment is a bad feeling and it's fine if you experience emotional stress. Rather than avoiding the emotion, you can just express the pain. You can scream at the top of your lungs, beat a pillow, or write something about your disappointment. However, never ever blame, dump, or hurt someone because you are disappointed. You just need to be honest with yourself, about what you really feel. Just express it so that you will be able to lighten the burden and move on to the next step.

The next thing to do is to put things into perspective. Initially, your disappointment can be really bad, and it is true that it may not be very easy to accept that you have worked hard to achieve a certain financial goal and yet you failed. The key here is to understand that while disappointment is a bad emotion, everyone can also feel it. Don't think that you are being punished or being singled out. You need to learn that disappointments don't last forever, just like other situations in life.

Is Fear of Disappointment Holding You Back?

Many of us grew up trying our best not to disappoint the people around us – our parents, teachers, relatives, and the society. This usually results in us making decisions that are based on a fear of disappointment. On the other hand, you may also try to avoid disappointing yourself.

You might have tried to promise something to do for yourself or for the people you care for, and you ended up not fulfilling that promise. This leads to a condition experts call "disappointment avoidance."

Neurologists and psychologists have collaborated in different studies to know more about this condition. They found out that each time people think about fulfilling a goal or try to do something they have failed in before (taking into account the pain caused by that failure), their memories send electrical signals to their brains, encouraging them to stop pursuing whatever it is they're trying to achieve.

This natural phenomenon happens to you because your brain tells you to avoid doing the same things that can lead to disappointment and thus could eventually hurt you. This is your body's natural mechanism to help you avoid risks and dangers. However, if you want to become successful and achieve your financial goals, you must try to fight disappointment avoidance. Many people have succeeded in never giving up. Don't let the fear of disappointment hold you back.

The key here is to think of what you are really avoiding and consider how you can take effective actions against it. This will help you keep moving forward and it can disrupt the neurological reactions of fear that is preventing you from achieving your goals.

Disappointment is Part of Success

Facing disappointment is part of the process of becoming successful. This is a painful experience that can teach you important life lessons. It can help you solidify your core, rebuild your character, and narrow down your focus. Along with disappointment comes pain, but it doesn't mean that any of those should be eliminated. We can use the lessons we have learned as stepping stones in reaching for success.

When you experience failure, get enough time to analyze what went wrong. It will be beneficial to evaluate what happened. Ask yourself questions, and be sure to specify the things that you think caused the failure.

Consider the story of Chris Bosh of the Miami Heat. He suffered injuries so he wasn't able to play in some playoffs in 2012. However, in an important game against Boston Celtics, he made three powerful three-point shots to the surprise of many, because Bosh was not actually a proficient three-pointer. He later explained that while he was not playing the game, he was watching the playoffs and he visualized how he could win and be successful.

Similar to Bosh, we also need to re-visualize our goals when we experience failure and disappointment. We need to see ourselves winning, accomplishing the most important goals. Will you allow your pain to hold you back? Will you sulk away in a corner to tend to your wounds forever? If you will do these things, you will just allow disappointment to destroy you and pin you down. How would you get up and accomplish your goals?

To overcome disappointment, you need to focus more on your most important goal. Be sure to write it down so that you will be clear on it. Writing down your goals will give you the clarity you need. To reach your goals, you should also commit yourself to doing tasks one step at a time. You can record your financial goals to help you visualize your commitment. Thinking about your motivation will also remind you of the reasons why you have established your goals. It can help you monitor and reinvigorate your efforts in pursuing your goals.

Take note that you should let go of the bad feelings that are holding you back. Everyone can experience disappointments, but successful people face the negative emotions and learn from the experience. After a painful experience, such as being disappointed, don't let yourself be pinned down, instead grow and learn from it.

Have a Mentor Standing By

Another important step in dealing with disappointments as well as in achieving your financial freedom is to have a mentor by your side. When you are looking for your financial mentor, you are basically looking for a way to be guided in navigating a mysterious terrain.

Searching for your mentor reveals your desire to improve your situation. This is crucial because, with the right person to ask assistance from, you can put yourself in a more favorable setting and thus be certain that you will not work as hard several decades from now to achieve financial security, financial comfort, and eventually, limitless wealth.

In searching for your financial mentor, choose one who doesn't merely have professional experience and training, but one who can steer you towards financial freedom. You must find someone who can be your partner, yet at the same time act like an integral part of your mind, that's devoted to helping you survive. With today's financial hardships, your mentor must help you survive by focusing on a number of assets in your investment portfolio.

Be Kind to Yourself

As mentioned above, it is never okay to play the blame game. You can vent out your anger or disappointment when you experience failure, but this doesn't mean that you can unleash your feelings on other people and hurt them physically or emotionally. This rule also applies to yourself.

Don't blame yourself for being disappointed or for failing to achieve your goals. Never hurt yourself and never think that you are a failure. You might have failed to fulfill a goal you have established yourself, but never think that it happened because you are not good. Rather, have the courage to introspect and ask yourself what went wrong. Through self-evaluation, you can learn how to conquer bad feelings as well as the pain. Don't be too hard on yourself. Instead, adjust your habits, your way of thinking, and your practices so that you could eventually achieve your goals.

Tell the Truth

Truth-telling will always have its victims. Be it yourself, your partners, or the people whom you care for, they may feel bad when they learn about the failures you are experiencing. There is veracity in the adage that truth-telling will set you free. That is right. When you say the truth, you are freeing yourself from pain as well as from the other bad feelings that come with disappointment, such as fear and anxiety.

Always be true not only to other people, such as your partners or mentor, but also to yourself. When you are true to yourself, you acknowledge the reality that you are a mere human capable of failing goals, but also capable of moving on and becoming much stronger. Dark alleys of lies need not cover the way towards financial freedom. Instead, it must be a clear way where you can see the sun shining bright as if guiding your way to your goals. Always tell the truth and you will be rewarded

Success and the Power of Belief

Being firm in what you believe in has a huge impact on how you achieve success. Once you believe that you will eventually succeed or finally grab what you desire, you certainly will succeed. The way you believe in yourself is like software codes that instruct your mind to energize the body and your will, so that you can achieve what you want. This is the actual power of believing. Your mind can respond to what you believe in and will work to create what you believe will happen.

To work properly with mind power and to instruct your mind, you need to have beliefs that are aligned with what you want. The things you believe will happen are what you will achieve. Your mind will pick up on your beliefs so you need to fill your mind with positive and great thoughts about being able to achieve your goals.

Your mind will create your life based on what you believe. Hence, take a closer look atwhat you believe in and start changing those beliefs, so that you send the right message to your mind. As a result, you will turn your aspirations into reality.

Never say to yourself that you can't do something. This will be like saying that you don't believe that you can reach whatever it is that you want to achieve. Your mind will pick this idea and will create the situations that will make it more difficult for you to succeed. Of course, you want to succeed, but it will be harder if you don't believe that you can. Hence, you need to change the way you believe in things, or else you will just continue the struggle and you will fail to achieve your financial goals.

Determine Success

We measure success in varied ways and on varied levels. In establishing your goals in life, it is crucial that you determine what success means to you personally, so that you will know if you have finally achieved your goals.

For instance, many people determine success in their personal finances according to their total savings. However, this may not be a very precise measurement. If you have enough savings but still you are not happy with your life because you have a job that you don't like, could that be considered successful?

Meanwhile, if you are measuring your success in achieving the goal of becoming rich, then your savings may not be an accurate indicator. Being clear on what you expect from yourself, in advance, provides you a way of keeping track of your progress.

For some people, being successful in business includes not only finding value in what they do but also sharing this vision with other people. Hence, aside from focusing on profit and enjoyment, you must also find a way to know if you are actually creating value for your partners, mentors, and other people to whom you have shared your financial freedom.

Once you set goals in any aspect of life, you need to identify early on what your expected results are and how you will know if you have finally reached your target. Being clear onwhat success looks like beforehand, will give you the chance to adjust your mindset with the right feelings – particularly those that success can provide. This will create a level of excitement that will eventually help you take the actions you need to achieve your goals.

Conclusion

Thank you again for downloading this book!

I hope this book was able to help you to understand the important techniques that can help you with financial freedom. I hope that you have also become aware of the different options available to you so you can build your portfolio and generate a financial plan to achieve this goal.

Finally, if you enjoyed this book, then I'd like to ask you for a favor, would you be kind enough to leave a review for this book on Amazon? It'd be greatly appreciated!

Click here to leave a review for this book on Amazon!

Thank you and good luck!

www.ingramcontent.com/pod-product-compliance
Lightning Source LLC
Chambersburg PA
CBHW070332190526
45169CB00005B/1856